NATURAL WORLD

GORILLA

HABITATS • LIFE CYCLES • FOOD CHAINS • THREATS

Stephen Brend

HODDER
Wayland

an imprint of Hodder
Children's Books

WWF

Produced in Association with WWF-UK

NATURAL WORLD

Chimpanzee • Crocodile • Black Rhino • Dolphin • Elephant • Giant Panda
Giraffe • Golden Eagle • Gorilla • Great White Shark • Grizzly Bear
Hippopotamus • Killer Whale • Koala • Leopard • Lion • Orangutan
Penguin • Polar Bear • Tiger • Wolf • Zebra

Produced for Hodder Wayland by
Roger Coote Publishing
Gissing's Farm, Fressingfield
Suffolk IP21 5SH, UK

Produced in association with WWF-UK.
WWF-UK registered charity number
1081247. A company limited by guarantee
number 4016725. Panda device © 1986 WWF.
® WWF registered trademark owner.

Cover: A male mountain gorilla up close.
Title page: An adult mountain gorilla eating.
Contents page: An adolescent gorilla demonstrating the characteristic 'knuckle walk'.
Index page: An adult gorilla relaxes in some late afternoon sun.

Published in Great Britain in 2002 by Hodder Wayland,
an imprint of Hodder Children's Books
Text copyright © 2002 Hodder Wayland
Volume copyright © 2002 Hodder Wayland

Editor: Steve Parker
Series editor: Victoria Brooker
Designer: Victoria Webb
Text consultant: Ian Redmond

British Library Cataloguing in Publication Data
Brend, Stephen
Gorilla. - (Natural World)
Gorilla - Juvenile literature
I.Title
599.8'84

ISBN 0 7502 3975 1

Printed and bound by G. Canale & C.S.p.A., Turin, Italy

Hodder Children's Books
A division of Hodder Headline Limited
338 Euston Road, London NW1 3BH

Picture acknowledgements
Ardea 31 Andrew Warren; *Bruce Coleman Collection* 7
Jorg & Petra Wegner, 36 Staffan Widstrand, 40 Mark
Carwardine; *Corbis* 3 Kennan Ward, 10 Gallo Images,
26 Karl Ammann, 35 Adrian Arbib; *Greg Cummings*
32; *Digital Vision* front cover, 45 middle, 48; *FLPA* 42
P Ward, 43 Roger Tidman; *Dian Fossey* 41; *NHPA* 11
Michael Leach, 15 Michael Leach, 24 Kevin Schafer,
25 Martin Harvey, 30 Martin Harvey, 38 Martin
Harvey, 44 middle Michael Leach; *Oxford Scientific
Films* 27 Andrew Plumptre, 45 bottom Andrew
Plumptre; *Ian Redmond* 1, 6, 8, 9, 12, 13, 14, 16, 17, 18,
20, 21, 22, 23, 28, 29, 33, 34, 37, 39, 44 top, 44 bottom,
45 top. Artwork by Michael Posen.

Contents

Meet the Gorilla 4

A Gorilla is Born 8

Growing Up 12

Leaving Home 20

A Day in the Group 28

Adult Life 32

Threats 36

Gorilla Life Cycle 44

Topic Web 46

Glossary 47

Further Information 47

Index 48

Meet the Gorilla

Gorillas are huge! They are the largest and strongest apes, easily able to kill a leopard. Yet they are gentle, peaceful plant-eaters.

There are several types of gorillas. All live in West and Central Africa. Some live in lowlands and some in high mountain forests. Mountain gorillas are very rare and are found only in the Virunga Volcanoes region of Central Africa.

AFRICA

▲ The red shading on this map shows where gorillas live in Africa.

GORILLA FACTS

A full-grown adult male gorilla stands almost 2 metres tall and may weigh more than 200 kilograms (the same as 3–4 adult humans). An average adult female weighs 120–130 kilograms and stands about 1.2 metres tall.

●

There are two kinds, or species, of gorilla. One is the Eastern gorilla, *Gorilla beringei*. It has three subgroups, or subspecies – mountain gorilla, bwindi gorilla and Eastern lowland gorilla.
The second species is the Western gorilla, *Gorilla gorilla*. It has two subspecies – Western lowland gorilla and Cross River gorilla.

Head
A male gorilla has an almost triangular head with a bony crest along the top of the skull, a ridge over the eyes, and powerful jaws. A female has a smaller, more rounded head.

Teeth
Near the front of the mouth are sharp canine teeth for tearing plants. In an adult male, these teeth are especially large, for threatening enemies. At the back of the mouth are broad molars for grinding food.

Hair and skin
The fur and skin are black, although some gorillas develop a reddish head-cap. Mountain gorillas have longer hair than other types. The face, ears, hands and feet lack hair.

Silverback
Adult male gorillas develop a band of silver-grey hair on the back. This gives them the name 'silverback'.

Legs
These are thicker but shorter than the arms, to support the massive body weight.

Hands
Gorilla hands are like ours – they have fingerprints, fingernails, and a flexible or opposable thumb to grasp objects. The fingers are thick and muscular. A gorilla on all fours walks on its knuckles, not on the palms of its hands.

Feet
A gorilla's big toe is less thumb-like than in other apes. But it can still grasp objects such as food or branches.

Habitat

Mountain gorillas live in a special type of tropical forest with short, moss-covered trees and patches of grasses, including tall bamboo. Some of the flowers are giants of their kind. The weather is cool or cold. Even in the dry season, it rains almost every day – but not quite as much as in the wet season.

▼ The volcanic Virunga Region of Central Africa rises over 4,000 metres above sea level. The forests found on the higher slopes are cooler and less dense than those lower down.

Relatives

Gorillas are great apes. This group also includes chimpanzees and orangutans. Their more distant relatives are gibbons and monkeys. All of these, along with lemurs, bushbabies and lorises, make up the mammal group known as primates.

The distant ancestors of great apes probably lived in Africa 20 million years ago. Orangutans branched from the family tree first, moving to South-east Asia. Gorillas were next, then chimpanzees and bonobos. This left another 'great ape' – humans. A gorilla's genes (the material which makes up the body) are almost identical to the genes of a human.

▲ Gorillas and humans are descended from the same common ancestor. We still share many of the same features, such as body shape, hands, feet and forward-facing eyes.

FRIGHTENING OR PEACEFUL?

Early European explorers in Africa told terrifying stories of fearsome giant apes that attacked people on sight. From the 1960s gorillas have been observed in their natural habitat. They are quiet, gentle and peaceful, but they can defend themselves if needed.

A Gorilla is Born

▼ A baby gorilla clings to its mother as she lies in a nest of leaves and branches.

Gorillas can be born at any time of the year, but the birth is usually at night. Most gorilla mothers have only one baby at a time. The birth occurs in a nest in the branches. If it takes a long time, the mother may make more nests and move from one to another. The tiny newborn gorilla is often covered in blood. The mother cleans it carefully, then it drinks her milk for the first time.

The baby gorilla is completely helpless. It can hold on to its mother with its hands and feet, but it depends on her for food, warmth and shelter. The mother holds the baby tightly to her chest when travelling, and on her lap as she feeds. The baby sleeps for much of the day, even as the mother moves around. It suckles very often, but takes only a little milk each time, each session lasting less than a minute. The baby grows very quickly – at least twice as fast as a human baby.

▲ A baby gorilla lies on its mother's chest and suckles her milk.

NEW-BORN GORILLA

A new-born gorilla has grey-pink skin with only small patches of hair. Its arms and legs are very thin. It is smaller than a new human baby, weighing only 2 kilograms.

First weeks

The gorilla baby stays within reach of its mother for at least six months. The mother usually carries it clasped to her front, as the gorilla group moves around. As the baby becomes bigger and stronger, it rides on its mother's back. This is a safe place, and also the mother has her arms free to climb, walk and run.

The gorilla mother sometimes plays with her baby. She swings it through the air or rolls it around her lap. This behaviour strengthens the bond between baby and mother, which is important. A young gorilla will stay close to its mother for many years.

▲ As the young gorilla gets stronger it will start to ride on its mother's back. It can see more of its surroundings and learn about the forest from this vantage point.

THREATS TO THE YOUNG

Perhaps the main danger to a young gorilla comes from its own kind. A new and powerful adult male gorilla may take over its group – and kill the babies. These were the offspring of the previous chief male, not his own.

A baby gorilla has few natural enemies. The massive adult gorillas in its group put off predators such as leopards. However a big cat may snatch an injured gorilla, and a python could take a baby that has wandered from its mother.

▼ A mother gorilla will not let her baby out of reach until it is over six months old.

Growing Up

A young gorilla grows fast and learns quickly. Its first teeth appear at the age of three months. It begins to try different types of foods, and copies what its mother eats. The youngster starts to eat solid food properly at about six months old. Even so, it still depends on its mother's milk.

Like human babies, most young gorillas learn to crawl before they can walk. As they try to walk for the first time, their legs wobble and bend, and they collapse in a small heap, squealing for their mothers. But they gain strength and coordination. By six months of age, they are playing happily near their mothers.

NOSE-PRINTS

People studying gorillas quickly learn to tell them apart by their nose-prints. This is the shape of the ridges and folds of skin above the nostrils. Each gorilla has a different nose-print.

◀ Young gorillas begin to explore their environment when they are six or seven months old. Some of the first foods they try are their mother's leftovers.

12

▶ Play is an important part of a young gorilla's development. Here, the silverback lets a youngster play around him.

Play is very important during these early months. Youngsters in the group chase and wrestle each other. They even play with the adults, jumping on them and play-biting. This helps to build a young gorilla's confidence. Compared to big groups, baby gorillas who grow up in small groups with fewer playmates tend to be more shy, and develop more slowly.

Food and nests

Young gorillas stop taking their mother's milk, and move onto solid foods, at about two years of age. This is called weaning. It is a stressful time because the young gorilla does not seem to understand why its mother begins to lose interest. The two hold each other and play together much less.

Even after the young gorilla is weaned, it still stays near its mother. It follows her on foot, and may climb onto her back for a short time, if it is tired or frightened. But it is now too heavy to carry long distances.

▲ Young gorillas begin eating a few plants and vegetables at about six months old. After weaning, at about two years of age, the youngster will depend entirely on the food it gathers itself.

GORILLA NESTS

A gorilla nest is a platform or bowl of stems, twigs, leaves and branches, in a tree or on the ground. The gorilla bends them over and twists, weaves or knots them together. A day-nest is for dozing. The night-nest is bigger and stronger, for sleeping. Each nest is used only once.

From the age of 18 months, the young gorilla practises making day-nests. Its first attempts are clumsy and untidy, as it simply pulls over a few grass stems! At night the youngster still shares its mother's night-nest, until she has her next baby.

▼ Gorillas grow rapidly. By the time they are three years old, they may already weigh 20 kilograms.

Juvenile gorillas

Gorillas are called juveniles when they are more than three years old. They no longer depend on their mothers. They move about and find food on their own. However a juvenile usually stays close to its mother, and may run to her if scared. It also still sleeps in her nest, if she has not had another baby. If she has a baby, the juvenile builds its own night-nest very close to its mother.

▼ Juvenile gorillas spend a lot of time close to their mothers. The strong attachment between them will last even after she has another baby.

A baby gorilla has a tuft of white hair on its backside. This acts as a sign to older gorillas, to treat the baby gently. As a gorilla becomes a juvenile, it loses this white hair. At this stage, male and female juveniles are similar in size and weight.

The juvenile gorilla likes climbing. It is smaller and lighter than an adult. So it can climb into trees more easily, to search for juicy leaves which are out of reach of the adults.

▲ Juvenile gorillas can be playful and boisterous and they climb trees far more often than adults. Here one sits on an overgrown tree stump.

◀ Gorilla groups spend most of the day together, always moving, eating and resting in sight of one another. When the group rests the adults relax while the youngsters play around them.

▶ Adult gorillas are at the top of their food chain and have no natural predators.

The gorilla group

Gorilla groups vary in size. A mountain gorilla group may number from five to twenty. In a typical group there is one chief or dominant male, the silverback. There are also one or two younger males known as blackbacks, and three or four adult females with their offspring. Strong bonds exist between the group members.

Food

Mountain gorillas eat plants – mainly leaves, bark, stems and vines – and not much fruit. They eat more than 150 different types of plants. They are very fond of certain wild vegetables, such as wild celery. Rarely, they may eat ants or grubs. But they do not seem to eat small animals such as lizards or birds.

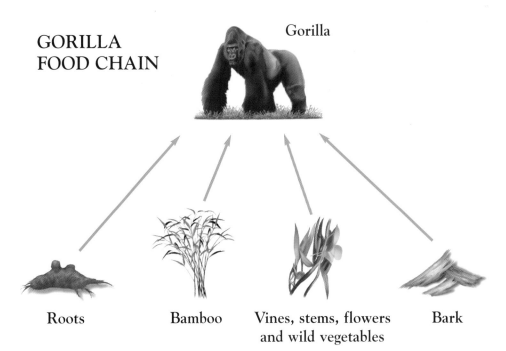

GORILLA
FOOD CHAIN

Gorilla

Roots   Bamboo   Vines, stems, flowers   Bark
                                 and wild vegetables

Leaving Home

At about six years of age, gorillas enter adolescence – the time when they develop into mature adults.

Differences now show between the sexes. Both males and females continue to put on weight, until they are about ten. But males keep growing taller, while females do not.

Adolescent females are able to breed from about eight years of age. However, most females have their first babies just before they are ten years old. By this time, they have usually moved away from their mother and joined another group.

▲ Until they are six years old, it is hard to tell male and female gorillas apart. However, once they enter adolescence, males begin to look much larger.

ADOLESCENCE

At about six years of age, both male and female gorillas are some 1.2 metres tall and weigh around 70 kilograms.

Adolescent males, called blackbacks, are too young to breed. They remain in their group, but they must be more and more careful around the dominant male, the silverback. He guards the females in his group against the blackbacks, even though they may be his own sons. However the family ties remain strong. The silverback may need the support of the blackbacks, to chase off gorillas from rival groups.

▲ This picture shows the difference between an adult and an adolescent male. The silverback on the left has developed the huge crowned head which is characteristic of a fully grown male.

21

The new silverback

A male gorilla becomes fully grown and able to breed between the ages of 11 and 13 years. At this time he grows the distinctive silver-grey hair across his back. Once this happens the silverback in his group, who may be his father, usually chases him away. However, if the old silverback is weak or ill, the young silverback may take over the group. In some cases this happens peacefully. In other cases there is much fighting and screaming.

▲ A young solitary silverback stares intently across an open patch of ground. He is wary of meeting another group, as the dominant male may attack him.

A young silverback who has left his group may live alone for a time. But gorillas do not like to be alone. Several young silverbacks may join to form a bachelor group. But these all-male groups rarely last long. In time the young silverback will move on to look for a group where he can challenge the silverback in charge. Or he may try to start a group of his own.

SOUNDS AND SMELLS

Gorillas make at least 25 different sounds, each with its own meaning. There are happy sounds like chuckling or belching, and angry sounds such as pig-like grunts and screams. Gorillas also use smell to communicate. They give off different odours depending on their mood.

▼ Gorillas make different sounds and have a variety of facial expressions. This young male is laughing!

Changing groups

Like male gorillas, females who become adults also leave the group where they were born. Unlike a young male, the young female rarely lives alone for any length of time. She usually joins another group straight away. This often happens when she senses that there is another group of gorillas close by. In most cases these exchanges happen peacefully. She is welcomed by the silverback of the other group.

▼ Female gorillas usually move away from their birth-group before they have the first baby. However, they may only change groups once in their lives.

▲ A silverback can not hold his group together by size and strength alone. He must also be popular with his females.

Sometimes, young females seem to be 'kidnapped'! A young silverback charges into the group and chases out one or two females to stay with him. This is one way that a new gorilla group can form. However, the females may not be willing. The new silverback must earn their trust and respect, or they may leave him. Some females change groups two or three times, before they settle down.

INBREEDING

Young adult female gorillas move away from the group because the silverback, who is the only male that breeds, is likely to be their father. If closely related animals breed, their offspring may be weak or not formed properly. This is called inbreeding.

A new leader

When one silverback challenges another for leadership of a group, the two carry out aggressive displays. They pick up sticks, pull branches, make noises and charge around, trying to frighten each other. They try to bite one another using their sharp canine teeth, screaming all the time. They may suffer horrific injuries, such as cuts to the face, neck, shoulders and arms, or broken bones. Very occasionally they die from their wounds.

▲ Gorillas are very powerful and they will use their large, sharp teeth for fighting. A silverback will show his teeth as a warning.

Not only the silverbacks suffer in such a battle. If a new silverback takes over a group, he is likely to kill all the babies and youngsters. If a mother gorilla has a baby, she cannot become pregnant again until the baby is weaned. But if she loses the baby, she can become pregnant again soon. By killing the babies, the new silverback makes sure that he will be the father of all the offspring in his group.

THE SILVERBACK'S CHARGE

A silverback beats his chest, roars and charges towards a threat, mouth open to reveal his huge teeth. The effect is terrifying. However, many charges are just for show. Gorillas do not like to fight. They try to scare their enemies into running away.

▼ This silverback is showing a threatening posture. The tension in his body shows he is ready to charge.

A Day in the Group

The gorilla's life is based around food, rest and sleep. As soon as they wake up and leave their night-nests, the gorillas begin to look for food. The group members tend to spread out, so they do not squabble over the same items. After the morning feed, they relax. Some make small day-nests where they doze. This is usually the time when the youngsters play.

▶ Eating is the most important daily activity for gorillas. The group feeds together, with the different individuals spread out over a patch of succulent grasses. This young gorilla is eating wild celery.

▲ The plants that make up the bulk of the gorillas' diet take a long time to digest. The group therefore rests after each big meal.

Mountain gorillas have plenty of food all around them. So they do not need to move very far. They may travel less than 400 metres each day. They move further when food is scarce, or if they want to reach a certain patch of forest where the plants are ripe.

The silverback shows the group which way to travel. Usually, the blackbacks are at the front, and the silverback brings up the rear. This ensures the females and young are well protected. A group with youngsters tends to travel more slowly than a group of adults or adolescents.

BIG APPETITE

Gorillas eat a lot of food every day. A male gorilla can eat as much as 30 kilograms, which is about one-sixth of his whole body weight.

Fussy eaters

After a midday nap, the gorillas feed again. Once more, they spread out and look for certain plants. They are very choosy and spend much time preparing the food before chewing it. They may pull leaves off branches, or strip juicy pieces from stems. They even crouch down and use their teeth to pull up small plants and roots from the ground.

◀ Grooming is a relaxed activity that may involve three or four gorillas at a time.

Home range

A gorilla group moves around an area called its home range. This is quite small compared to the home ranges of other apes, such as chimps. It may be only 400 hectares, although some groups have larger areas. The home ranges of nearby groups may join each other, but the gorillas rarely defend their home range by chasing out other groups. If one group comes close to another, usually by chance, the silverback becomes uncomfortable. He may move his group to a safe distance. No matter where they have been feeding by day, the group always moves to a new area, to rest for the night.

▶ Adult gorillas are usually too heavy to spend much time climbing trees. Here though, an adult female runs along a strong branch.

Adult Life

In a gorilla group, only the silverback mates with the females. He has usually become a father by the age of fifteen. Each female can be ready to mate at any time of year, but only for a short period each month. She tries to attract all the males in the group, however the silverback chases them away. The courtship between silverback and female is usually very brief.

▼ A silverback beats his chest before launching into a charge. The 'pok-pok' noise of the chest beating can be heard over 200 metres away.

 A mature female gorilla usually has her first baby at about the age of 10 years.

PREGNANCY

A female gorilla is pregnant (expecting a baby) for eight-and-a-half months. Because gorillas have large bellies, it is sometimes difficult for people studying them to judge if a female is pregnant. Usually, her change in behaviour is more obvious than her change in shape.

Early in her pregnancy, the female becomes interested in other babies in the group. The experienced mothers let her hold and play with their offspring. In this way, the young female learns the skills of being a mother. A typical female usually has a baby every three-and-a-half to four years. Once a new baby arrives, her older offspring is kept out of the night-nest. But the bond between mother and older offspring remains strong for several more years.

Seniors and juniors

The silverback is the clear leader of a gorilla group. However, the rank or importance of other members is less clear. Younger males may be bold and try to bully the females, but the silverback keeps them under strict control. Among the females, the older ones seem to be higher in rank than the younger ones. However the silverback is very protective of any female with a baby.

◀ Adult gorillas have few natural enemies. Their size and the presence of the other group members prevent predators, such as leopards, attacking them.

▶ As gorillas age, their teeth wear down. This makes eating more difficult and they start to lose weight.

Growing old

No one knows for certain how long gorillas live. Probably, nearly half of them die before they become adults. A silverback is unlikely to be older than about 35 years. By this age, life becomes tough, and he may be attacked by a younger, stronger rival. Also gorillas often lose their teeth as they age. This makes eating difficult and so an old gorilla becomes thin and weak.

THE END

Most gorillas do not die from attacks by predators. They fall victim to diseases such as pneumonia or the infection of an old wound.

Threats

Mountain gorillas are 'critically endangered' – they may die out completely within ten years. There are probably around 600 left in the Virunga region. The main threat to them is illegal hunting and loss of habitat. In many parts of Africa, including Virunga, people catch and kill wild animals to eat. It's called the bushmeat trade. It is against the law to kill gorillas, but this does not stop hunters with dogs, guns and spears. The meat from the gorilla's body is eaten. Its head or hands may be turned into horrible trinkets or souvenirs, such as ashtrays.

THE RAREST GORILLAS

Cross River gorillas are the most endangered. There may be only 200 left.

▼ The male in this picture was later killed by poachers when he tried to defend his group.

▲ Snares set for other animals sometimes catch gorillas. This blackback male lost his hand to a snare but still managed to survive. He learnt to use his stump to help him eat.

Some hunters set snares made from loops of twisted wire. They hope to catch small mammals such as forest antelopes. But a gorilla may be caught instead. It could lose a finger or toe, or even a whole hand or foot, as the sharp wire tightens. Some gorillas die from such injuries.

If a group is attacked, the silverback will try to defend his group and is often the first to be killed. With their leader gone, the rest of the group may scatter. Even if they escape the hunters, they are unlikely to survive on their own.

Nowhere to live

Another great threat to mountain gorillas is loss of their habitat – the high forests where they live. Ever since the Virunga National Park was created, people have tried to graze their cattle inside its boundaries. People also cut down trees for use as firewood. This greatly alters the gorillas' homeland.

▼ On the slopes of the Virunga Mountains, the forest is cleared by people collecting firewood or to make way for farms. Sometimes the gorillas raid these plantations, which makes them unpopular with the farmers.

▲ After the civil war in Rwanda, in 1994, huge refugee camps like this one sprang up right on the very edge of the National Park in which the mountain gorillas live. The refugees would go into the park to collect firewood. Some even hunted the gorillas for food.

In 1994 there was a terrible war in Rwanda. Almost one million people fled from the country, and many of them went across the Virunga region. Thousands lived in camps at the base of the mountains. They went into the park to find firewood, shelter and food – and some killed gorillas. For safety, the other gorilla groups moved even higher up the mountains. At such great height, it is colder and wetter, and the gorillas face a bigger risk of disease.

The pet trade

Young gorillas are sometimes sold as pets to tourists or animal dealers. To capture a baby gorilla, hunters must first shoot its mother, and often the group's silverback as well. The group may not survive, and the baby gorilla is greatly distressed. Many babies soon die. The whole process is against the law.

Saving gorillas

One of the main ways to save gorillas is to protect their habitat. Conservation groups from many different countries work with the governments of Rwanda, Uganda and the Democratic Republic of the Congo, to protect the gorillas and the Virunga National Park.

▼ A ranger patrol keeps watch on a large silverback. Poachers may be very aggressive and are often armed with guns. Some rangers have been killed trying to defend the gorillas.

► A snare wound on the foot of a young gorilla. If they don't get immediate treatment, gorillas with wounds like this are likely to die.

CAPTIVE BREEDING

Mountain gorillas are too rare, and their social lives are too complicated, to save them by captive breeding. This is when animals are captured, bred in zoos or wildlife parks, and released back into the wild. There are no mountain gorillas in zoos anywhere in the world.

The International Gorilla Conservation Programme also provides much help, including support for the wildlife rangers. The rangers try to keep poachers and cattle farmers away from the park and the gorillas.

There is also a veterinary health clinic for the gorillas. The vets help a gorilla to recover if it has been caught in a snare. The surgeons give the gorilla medicines, remove the snare and treat its wounds, before releasing it back to its group.

Ecotourism

Many tourists want to visit the gorillas. When tourists travel to see wildlife, without disturbing it, this is called ecotourism. It brings much-needed money to countries like Rwanda, and it has helped save mountain gorillas. Most of the money from the tourists is used to pay the rangers and other park staff.

▼ Some gorillas have become used to people being around them. Because they do not run away they are easier to guard and scientists can study them up close.

▲ Rangers and trackers are recruited from among the local people. They have a lot of knowledge about the gorilla's range and are most able to protect them.

Specially trained guides take small groups of tourists up into the mountains. They quietly watch certain gorilla groups, which are used to people. The gorillas do not run away. In fact, as the visitors watch the gorillas, the gorillas appear to study the visitors!

Tourists must obey strict rules. They must not go nearer than five metres to the gorillas. Certainly, they must never touch them. This reduces the risk of the gorillas catching diseases from people.

Education

Helping people to learn about wildlife, forests and gorillas also saves the gorillas. Local people find out how they can live in ways which disturb the forests less, for example, by using less firewood. This is very important. No matter how many tourists come to the area, the future of the gorillas really lies with the people who share their mountain home.

Gorilla Life Cycle

 **1** A single gorilla baby is born after a pregnancy of eight-and-a-half months. The baby is born in its mother's night-nest. The baby develops its first teeth at three months old. It begins to eat solid foods from six months of age.

 **2** By the time the gorilla is two years old, it is weaned and able to find all its own food. Male and female gorillas look very similar at this stage.

 **3** At the age of three, a young gorilla is called a juvenile. Its mother may have another baby around this time, so the juvenile begins to sleep in its own night-nest.

 A gorilla's adolescence, when it begins to grow into a mature adult, begins at the age of six. Adolescent males grow taller and start to look different from the females.

 An adult male gorilla develops his silver-grey back at the age of about 11–12 years. However he will probably not have a group of his own until 14–15 years old. A female gorilla usually has her first baby by the age of 10 years. She will then have another baby every three-and-a-half to four years.

 Once a silverback has his own group, he is the dominant male until another male takes over from him, or until he dies. Gorillas can live to be more than 35 years old.

Gorilla Topic Web

SCIENCE
- Rain forest and mountain habitats
- Food chains
- Classification and evolution of great apes
- Adaptations, parts of the body
- Gorillas spreading seeds in droppings
- Life cycle of a gorilla
- Interdependence of plants and animals

ENGLISH AND LITERACY
- Conservation debates
- Gorilla legends and myths

MATHS
- Height and weight comparisons
- Gorilla group sizes
- Population density and range size

ICT
- Search for gorilla-related websites
- Look up Rwanda and Uganda on the Internet

ART
- Drawing gorillas
- Bark and leaf pictures
- Gorilla masks

GEOGRAPHY
- Map work, where gorillas live
- Environmental change and habitat destruction
- Mountain weather, seasons and rainfall
- Ecotourism

Extension Activities

English
- Debate the pros and cons of keeping endangered species in zoos.
- Review films like *King Kong* to see what sort of image they give the gorilla.
- Write a letter to a conservation group expressing a point of view.

Geography
- Trace a map of the world to show where primates are found and where gorillas are found.

Maths
- Compare the numbers of mountain gorillas to people in each of the countries in which they are found.
- Compare the heights and weights of the different great apes.

Science
- Make a list of body parts that humans and gorillas share.
- Discuss the effect of tropical deforestation on both people and gorillas.
- Compare a gorilla's diet with a human diet.

Glossary

Adolescent The stage of an animal's life as it grows into a mature adult, able to breed.

Breed To produce young.

Canine teeth Large, sharp 'eye teeth' near the front of the jaw, used by gorillas for biting and fighting.

Courtship The behaviour of a male and female animal that leads to mating.

Dominant The leading animal in a group, usually the most powerful and aggressive.

Endangered Living things which are low in numbers, perhaps in danger of dying out altogether (extinction).

Habitat The natural place for an animal or plant.

Home range An area of land used by an animal or group. (It is not usually defended against others, as a territory is.)

Juvenile A gorilla is called a juvenile when it is between the ages of 4 and 8 years old.

Mammal A warm-blooded animal that has hair or fur, and feeds its young on mother's milk.

Opposable thumb A thumb positioned at an angle or opposite to the fingers, so the hand can grip strongly.

Predator An animal that hunts and kills other creatures.

Species A group of animals or plants that share similar features and can breed together to produce young.

Suckle To drink milk from a mother mammal's teats.

Weaning To stop drinking mother's milk and start eating solid foods.

Further Information

Organizations to Contact

WWF-UK
Panda House, Weyside Park
Godalming, Surrey GU7 1XR
Tel: 01483 426444
Website: www.wwf-uk.org

Dian Fossey Gorilla Fund
Europe
110 Gloucester Avenue
London NW1X 8HX
Tel: 020 7483 2681
Website: www.gorillas.org

Websites

The Ape Alliance
www.4apes.com
The Ape Alliance is made up of more than 30 conservation groups who work to save all great apes. Their website has lots of links to gorilla groups.

www.cotf.edu/ete/modules/
mgorilla/mgorilla.html
A resource site on mountain gorillas, for teachers.

Books to Read

Gorilla by Ian Redmond (Dorling Kindersley Eyewitness Guides, 1997)
Gorillas by Jill M Caravan (Todtri, 1999)
My Gorilla Journey by Helen Attwater (Sidgwick and Jackson, 1999)

Index

Page numbers in **bold** refer to photographs or illustrations.

apes 4, 5, 7, 31, 46

blackbacks 19, 21, 29, **37**
bwindi gorilla 4

chest beating 27, **32**
climbing 17, **17**, **31**
conservation 40, 41
Cross River gorillas 4, 36

diseases 35, 39, 43

Eastern gorilla 4
Eastern lowland gorilla 4

fighting 22, **26**, 47
food chain **19**, 46

Gorilla beringei 4
Gorilla gorilla 4

habitat loss 36, 38
hair 5, 9, 17, 22, 47
home range **31**, 47
hunters 36, 37, **39**

juveniles 16, **16**, 17, **17**, **44**, 47

milk 8, 9, **9**, 12, 14, 47
mountain gorillas 4, 5, 6, 19, 29, 36, 38, 39, 41, 42

nests 8, **8**, 15, 16, 28, 33, **44**
nose-prints 12

play 10, 12, **13**, 14, **17**, **19**, 28, 33
poachers **36**, 40, 41
pregnancy 27, 33, **44**
primates 7, 46

rangers **40**, 41, 42, **43**

sleep 9, 15, 16, 28, **44**
sounds 23, **23**
species 4, 47

teeth 5, 12, 26, **26**, 27, 35, **35**, **44**, 47
tourists 39, 42, 43

Western gorilla 4
Western lowland gorilla 4